Mysteries

Wright
Group

Contents

Was there treasure in this box?
PAGE **22**

Could the Yeti be real?
PAGE **4**

Will you ever meet an alien?
PAGE **27**

Is there really a huge creature hiding in the Himalayas?

Did someone bury treasure worth 20 million dollars?

Are aliens from outer space watching us?

MYSTERIES

CANADA

USA

SANTA FÉ

OAK ISLAND

EASTER ISLAND

SOUTH AMERICA

PAGE 22 *Beale Treasure*

Oak Island Treasure PAGE 19

Easter Island PAGE 14

What Is a **Mystery?**

Any occurrence that remains unclear or unknown is called a *mystery*.

Sometimes the ways and customs of ancient people seem mysterious because we do not understand them. Sometimes things that appeared mysterious to people long ago have very simple explanations now, and are not mysteries at all. Sometimes mysteries are exaggerated stories, made up after the real events have been forgotten.

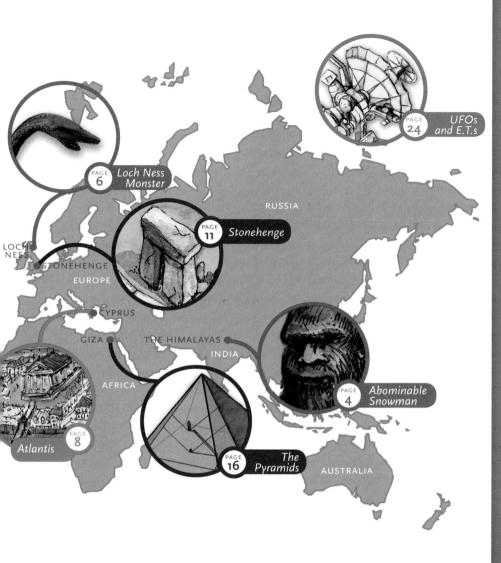

PAGE 24 — UFOs and E.T.s

PAGE 6 — Loch Ness Monster

RUSSIA

PAGE 11 — Stonehenge

LOCH NESS

STONEHENGE

EUROPE

CYPRUS

GIZA

THE HIMALAYAS

INDIA

AFRICA

PAGE 8 — Atlantis

PAGE 4 — Abominable Snowman

PAGE 16 — The Pyramids

AUSTRALIA

Can you solve the mysteries by looking at all the clues? What's your theory?

Unsolved Mysteries

Solving mysteries is like going on a treasure hunt or solving a jigsaw puzzle. Some people spend their lives hunting for the missing pieces. They have their own theories about why mysterious things happen. But without every piece of the puzzle, it's impossible to prove which theory is right. That's why many famous mysteries remain unsolved.

There's no such thing as a monster, right? Ever heard of the **Abominable** Snowman or the Loch Ness Monster? No one knows for sure if these monsters really exist, but **cryptozoologists** are on the case.

The *Abominable Snowman*

The Himalayan Mountain Range in Tibet is the highest mountain range in the world. It's also a very mysterious place. Some cryptozoologists believe that a hairy, human-like beast lives there. They call this beast the *Yeti*, or the *Abominable Snowman*. *Yeti* means *magical creature* in the Tibetan language.

Has Anyone Ever Seen the Monster?

The first reliable sighting of the Abominable Snowman was in 1925. A Greek photographer, N. A. Tombazi, was on a **trek**. He saw a giant creature moving in the distance.

THE HIMALAYAS

Machapuchare Peak in Nepal is part of the Himalayas.

It was a terrifying sight, but by the time Tombazi grabbed his camera, the creature had disappeared. It was only later that he found enormous footprints in the snow ... proof he hadn't imagined the monster.

In 1951, two frightened British trekkers thought they found the Yeti's footprints in the snow. The footprints measured 13 inches wide (33 centimeters) and 18 inches long (46 centimeters). With feet that big, imagine how huge a monster it must be!

Is the Abominable Snowman Real?

There are many unanswered questions about the Abominable Snowman. How can it live in such a cold and remote place? Is there more than one? If the creature is so huge, how has it stayed hidden for so long? What's your theory?

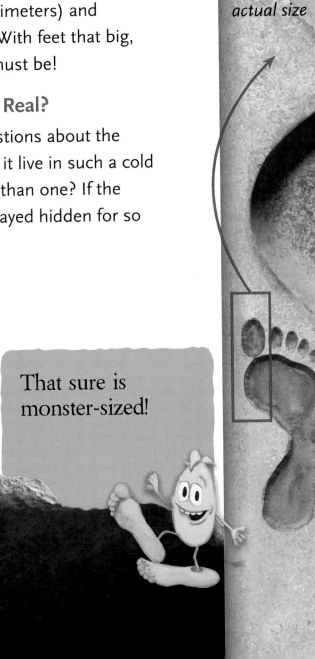

The mysterious footprint, drawn at actual size

That sure is monster-sized!

The Yeti, or Abominable Snowman, is still a mystery. Although many people have reported seeing it and its footprints, no one knows for sure if it really exists.

The **Loch Ness Monster**

Is this just a made-up story, or could a monster live in the deep, dark waters of a Scottish lake?

In 1933, someone reported seeing a monster swimming in the chilly waters of Loch Ness, a large lake in Scotland. This monster is known as the *Loch Ness Monster*, or *Nessie* for short.

What Does the Loch Ness Monster Look Like?

The Loch Ness Monster is reported to be a large dinosaur-like creature with two humps, a tail, and a snake-like head. It looks a bit like a pleiseosaur—a dinosaur that lived millions of years ago.

Is the Loch Ness Monster Real?

Over the years, many people claim to have seen the Loch Ness Monster. Some have even photographed it. But there is no scientific proof to say it is real. Many of the photos have since turned out to be fakes.

There have been many searches to find proof that Nessie exists. Several teams have tried to find it using **sonar** equipment. This equipment finds objects under water by bouncing sounds off them. The searches have bounced sounds off several unusual objects that may or may not be the creature.

a pleiseosaur

This sonar image was taken at Loch Ness. Do you think it's Nessie?

So the question remains. Could this monster be real: still alive from the time of dinosaurs? Or is it just an imaginary creature that never really existed?

LOCH NESS

Is Atlantis an ancient and magical lost city or another made-up story?

A LOST CITY
Atlantis

In 355 BC, a famous **philosopher** named Plato wrote about a magical island city called Atlantis.

Where in the World Was Atlantis?

Plato described Atlantis as an island bigger than all of Asia, and that the water surrounding Atlantis was named the Atlantic Ocean. These clues have led to searches near the Andes Mountains in Bolivia, off the coast of Florida, in Central America, in the China Sea, and even in Africa.

What Was Atlantis Like?

In his books, Plato described a wonderful land full of riches and great knowledge.

The people of Atlantis lived happy lives in peace and luxury. There were beautiful temples and palaces made from marble and covered in gold and silver. Cattle grazed in lush, green pastures, and drank from crystal clear streams full of fish. The markets were filled with delicious fruits and vegetables. The perfume from flower gardens filled the air. No wonder Atlantis is sometimes called a lost paradise.

Plato

What could have destroyed the beautiful city of Atlantis?

Was it flooded by a tidal wave?

A LOST CITY

What Happened to Atlantis?

Plato wrote that this magical island disappeared into the ocean in just one day and one night. We know today that such a catastrophe might have been caused by a natural disaster, like a tidal wave, a volcanic eruption, an earthquake, or a cyclone.

Did Atlantis really exist? People are still searching for the magical city today. Perhaps one day the ruins of beautiful Atlantis will be found.

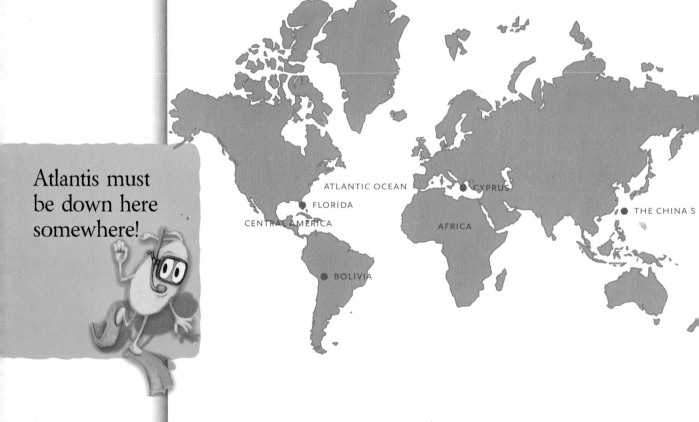

Atlantis must be down here somewhere!

ATLANTIC OCEAN

CYPRUS

FLORIDA

CENTRAL AMERICA

AFRICA

THE CHINA S

BOLIVIA

MYSTERIOUS ANCIENT STRUCTURES

There are strange, wondrous structures all over the world. Who built them and why? How were they built? What do they mean?

STONEHENGE

Stonehenge

Stonehenge is a circle of huge stones in southern England. Why and how it was built remains a mystery to this day, but there are many theories. Some people think that magical giants used their powers to build it. Others believe aliens from outer space built the circle as a landing area for their spacecraft. Or maybe, priests built it as a place of worship. Still other people think Stonehenge might have been used as a giant calendar to record the movements of the sun, moon, and stars.

Imagine carrying these huge stones using only muscle power, ropes, and wooden levers!

What Do We Know About Stonehenge?

We do know that Stonehenge is very old. It was built over 4,000 years ago.

We know it must have been very important to the people who built it. It took a long time to build and a lot of hard work.

We know that bluestone was used to build Stonehenge. Many of the larger stones weigh over 25 tons (22.7 tonnes) and were carried from a place 18 miles (29 kilometers) away.

This is how Stonehenge looked when it was first built over 4,000 years ago.

Imagine the interesting stories these stones could tell!

This is how Stonehenge looks today. It's different from when it was first built. Over time, much of the original bluestone has worn away, though some was taken to build homes and roads. Over the years, some of the remaining stones have been damaged by visitors.

Stonehenge still remains a magical and special place. Thousands of people from all over the world visit the stones, and wonder what mysteries and secret stories they hold about the past.

The giant, stone statues found on Easter Island have puzzled people for hundreds of years. What were they for? Why are they so huge? What happened to the people who built them?

Archaeologists are beginning to answer some of these questions.

Easter Island

Easter Island, located in the southern Pacific Ocean, is one of the most remote islands on Earth, and one of the most mysterious.

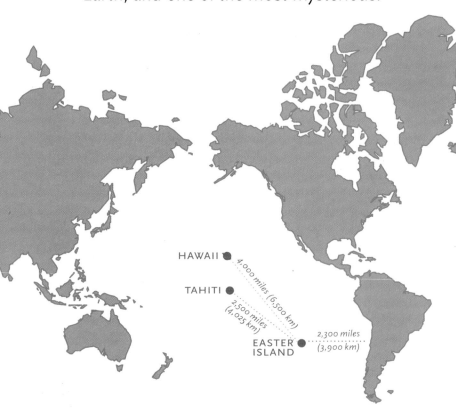

HAWAII

TAHITI

4,000 miles (6,500 km)

2,500 miles (4,025 km)

EASTER ISLAND

2,300 miles (3,900 km)

The people who discovered Easter Island must have been excellent sailors!

Stone Giants

At last count there were over 900 giant, stone heads on Easter Island. Archaeologists think ancient islanders carved the statues, called *moai*, to honor their leaders and gods. The largest moai, known as *El Gigante*, is 72 feet (22 meters) long, and it weighs over 150 tons (140 tonnes)! The moai were carved out of volcanic rock. Some of them were moved from the **quarry** where they were carved and placed on the shoreline. Many of the statues still stand there today, with their backs to the sea, as if they are watching over the villages and their people.

Moving a Giant!

One of the greatest mysteries about the stone giants is how they were moved from the quarry.

The ancient islanders didn't have cranes or trucks. So how did they haul the heavy heads?

Some islanders believe that a magical force called *mana* moved the statues. Others believe that they were rolled from the quarry on log rafts.

32 FEET
(9.8 METERS)

The tallest stone giant standing is 32 feet (9.8 meters) high and weighs 82 tons (83 tonnes)

5.5 FEET
(1.68 METERS)

No one really knows how or why the ancient people of Easter Island moved these huge, stone giants.
What do you think?

15

UNLOCK THE Mystery

Why did the Egyptians mummify people when they died?

MYSTERIOUS ANCIENT STRUCTURES

The **Pyramids** of **Egypt**

Pyramids are large structures with four triangular sides that meet in a point. The point sits directly over the center of the pyramid's square base.

Ancient pyramids can be found all over the world, but the largest and most famous pyramids are found in Egypt. They are called the *Pyramids of Giza*. These massive stone structures were built near the Nile river about 4,500 years ago.

Why Were the Pyramids Built?

Some people think that the ancient Egyptians built these pyramids as tombs for the pharaohs and their queens. The pharaohs were the rulers of ancient Egypt. After a ruler died, the ruler's body was carefully treated and wrapped to preserve it as a **mummy**. It was the hope of every Egyptian to be reborn after death.

Ancient Egyptians placed the mummies in the pyramids because they believed this was the way the rulers passed into the afterlife.

GIZA ●

How did the Egyptians lift over two million blocks of stone up to a height of 480 feet (146 meters), when each stone weighed over 2 tons (2 tonnes)?

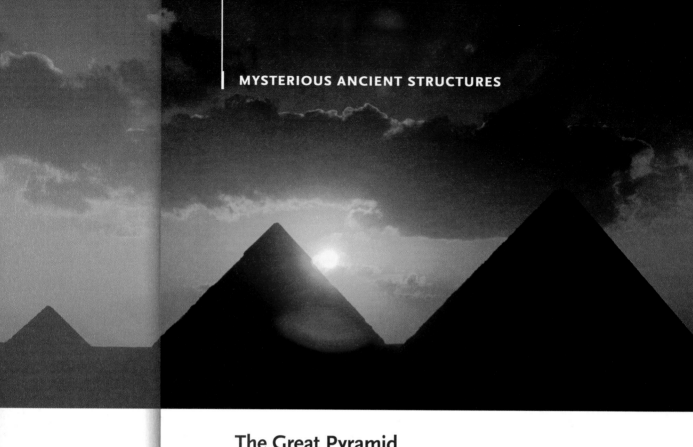

The Great Pyramid

The Great Pyramid is the best known of the Giza pyramids. It was built for the Pharaoh Khufu, or Cheops, as he was called. For centuries, it was the tallest structure on Earth. The ancient Greeks called the Great Pyramid one of the Seven Wonders of the World.

Petronas Twin Towers, *Malaysia*
1,483 feet (452 meters)

Empire State Building, *USA*
1,454 feet (443 meters)

Eiffel Tower, *France*
1,062 feet (323 meters)

Great Pyramid, *Egypt*
480 feet (146 meters)

Sydney Opera House
Australia
230 feet (70 meters)

2,500 BC   1899   1931   1973   2000

THE MYSTERY OF BURIED TREASURES

What would it be like to find a buried treasure? There are many famous stories about gold, silver, and jewels that have stayed hidden for hundreds or thousands of years. The treasures mentioned here have not yet been found—do they really exist, or are they legends?

OAK ISLAND ●

Oak Island

Daniel McGinnis's Discovery

In 1795, on Oak Island, Nova Scotia, a teenager named Daniel McGinnis discovered a large, sunken area in the ground.

Daniel knew that pirates like Captain Kidd and Blackbeard once sailed off the coast of Nova Scotia. Could it be he had discovered where these pirates had buried their treasure?

Over the next weeks, Daniel and his friends dug into the pit. First they found a layer of flagstone, a kind of rock not usually found in Nova Scotia. Then, every 10 feet (3 meters), they found a layer of oak logs. As they dug deeper, they realized they couldn't solve the mystery alone.

Soon the rumor spread that there was treasure to be found on Oak Island.

Blackbeard

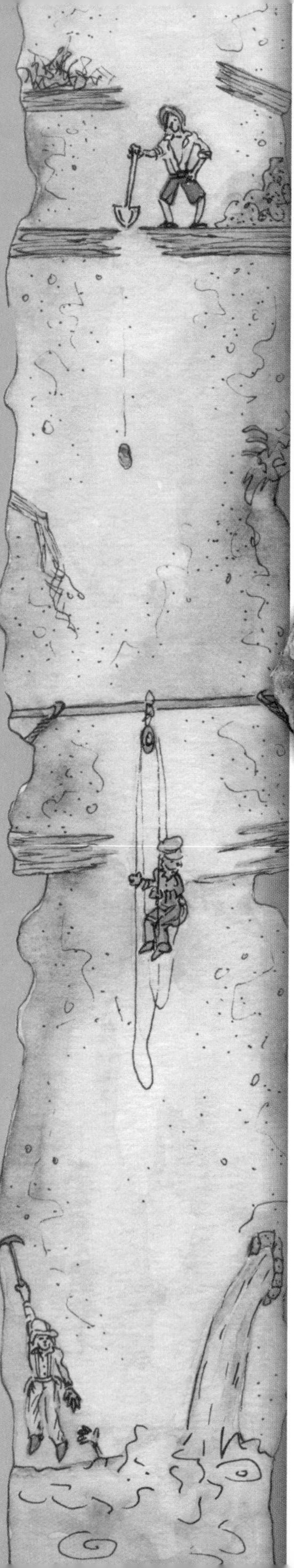

1795
Daniel McGinnis begins digging

1849
The Truro Company takes over

1861
The pit collapses while being explored by the Oak Island Association

Other treasure hunters and explorers joined the search over many years. Daniel's pit became known as the *Money Pit*. As they dug deeper into the pit, they found that it was blocked off every 10 feet (3 meters) by layers of oak logs, charcoal, coconut fiber, spruce, cement, and iron.

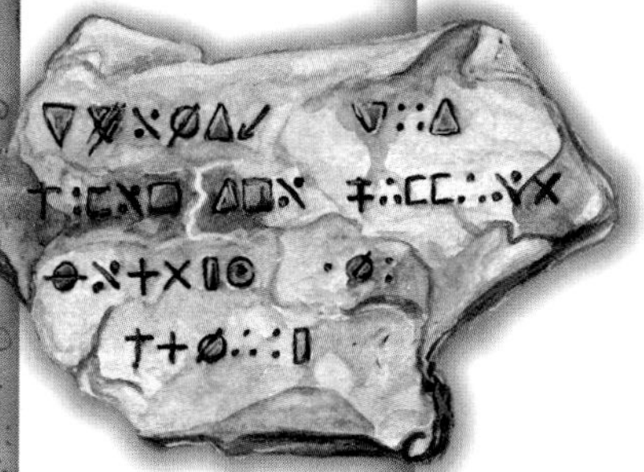

Clues

As different crews dug into the pit, they found clues about what might be buried there.

At a depth of 90 feet (27 meters), one crew found a large stone inscribed with strange letters.

At 153 feet (46 meters), another crew discovered a small piece of sheepskin **parchment** with the letters *ui*, *vi*, or *wi* written on it. Experts set to work to **decipher** the message. But so far no one has cracked the code.

Booby Trapped

One crew dug so far into the pit that it began to fill up with water. At a depth of 120 feet (37 meters), a tunnel was discovered that had been built from the sea to the pit.

This tunnel acted like a **booby trap** by flooding the pit with seawater and making it almost impossible to continue the dig. A **dam** was built, and dynamite was used to blast the tunnel to try and block the flow of water. But the pit continued to fill with water, as if it wanted to keep its secret safe forever.

A Gruesome Discovery

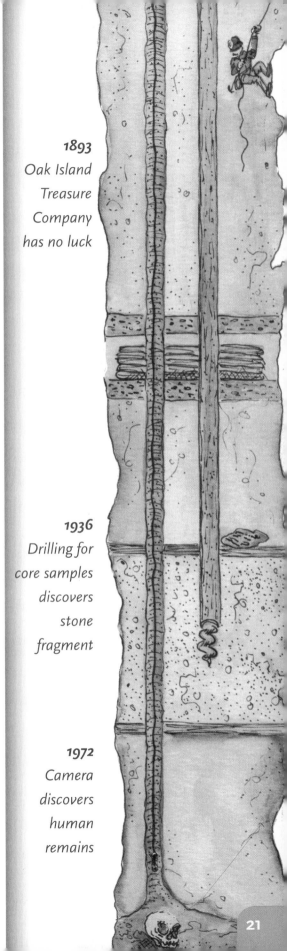

In 1972, an underwater camera was lowered into the pit to a depth of 230 feet (70 meters). The camera photographed what appeared to be logs and sea chests. Suddenly, to everyone's horror, the camera showed a human skull and a **severed** hand. Divers tried to retrieve these objects, but the pit collapsed and has never been reopened.

Daniel and his friends started a treasure hunt that has lasted over 200 years. Several people have died trying to solve the mystery of the Oak Island pit, but the treasure, if it exists, has yet to be discovered.

1893
Oak Island Treasure Company has no luck

1936
Drilling for core samples discovers stone fragment

1972
Camera discovers human remains

The *Beale* Treasure

The mystery of the Beale Treasure began in about 1820 in Virginia. Thomas Jefferson Beale asked his friend, Robert Morriss, to protect a locked iron box. Beale said the box contained "papers of value and importance." Morriss kept the locked box for over 23 years, but Beale never returned to collect it.

VIRGINIA ●
● SANTA FÉ

What Was in the Locked Box?

In 1845, Morriss lost his patience and cracked the box open. Inside was a note describing Beale's journey across America to hunt buffalo.

According to the note, one of Beale's men had unexpectedly struck gold near Santa Fé. They dug further, and quickly uncovered huge amounts of gold and silver. The men traded the gold and silver for jewels, and returned home rich men. To keep the jewels safe, Beale buried them somewhere in Virginia. But where?

Morriss was excited, but he needed more clues to solve the mystery. At the bottom of the box, he came across three papers covered with numbers.

Deciphering the Clues

The numbers were secret codes that told where the treasure could be found, but the code was too complicated to understand.

People have spent their whole lives trying to decipher the codes, and find the buried treasure. So far no one has succeeded. Maybe the Beale Treasure is just a **hoax**.

THE BEALE PAPERS

containing Authentic Statements regarding the **TREASURE BURIED** in 1819 and 1821, *near* Bufords, in Bedford County, Virginia, and **Which Has Never Been Recovered.**

nd Job Print 1885.

h the year 1885, by J. B. Congress, at Washington.

The Locality Of The Vault.

71, 194, 38, 1701, 89, 76, 11, 83, 1629, 48, 94, 63, 132, 16, 111, 95, 84, 341, 975, 14, 40, 64, 27, 81, 139, 213, 63, 90, 1120, 8, 15, 3, 126, 2018, 40, 74, 758, 485, 604, 230, 436, 664, 582, 150, 251, 284, 308, 231, 124, 211, 486, 225, 401, 370, 11, 1... 139, 189, 17, 33, 88, 208, ... 73, 416, 918, 263, ... 136, 21... 485, 1... 320, ... 961, ... 12, ... 486 ... 18 ... 4...

367, 460, 17, 81, 12, 103, 820, 62, 116, 97, 103, 862, 70, 60, 820, 62, 471, 540, 208, 121, 890, 1317, 150, 59, 568, 614, 13, 120, 63, 219, 812, 2160, 1780, 99, 35, 18, 21, 136, 872, 15, 28, 170, 88, 4, 30, 44, 112, 18, 147, 436, 195, 320, 37, 122, 113, 6, 140, 8, 120, 305, 42, 58, 461, 44, 106, 301, 13, 408, 680, 93, 86, 116, 530, 82, 568, 9, 102, 38, 416, 89, 71, 216, 728, 965, 818, 2, 38, 121, 195, 14, 326, 148, 234, 18, 55, 131, 234, 361, 824, 5, 81, 623, 48, 961, 19, 26, 33, 10, 1101, 365, 92, 88, 181, 275, 346, 201, 206, 86, 36, 219, 324, 829, 840, 64, 326, 19, 48, 122, 85, 216, 284, 919, 861, 326, 985, 233, 64, 68, 431, 960, 50, 29 ... 14, 612, 81, ... 78, 60, 200, ... 18, 61, 136, ... 664, 895, 10, ...

Codes are sometimes called *ciphers*. Now I know where the word *decipher* comes from—de_cipher, get it?

SAUCERS THAT FLY!

In 1947, an American pilot saw unusual flying objects over California. "They flew like saucers skipping over the water," he said. Since then, UFOS have often been called *flying saucers.*

MYSTERIES BEYOND OUR WORLD

The more we learn about our universe, the more mysterious it becomes. Is there life out there? If so, is it anything like ours?

UFOs

What is a UFO?

The letters UFO stand for *Unidentified Flying Object*. A UFO is something in the sky that cannot be named or explained. Many people think that UFOS are alien ships from outer space.

UFO Sightings

In 1947 in Kentucky, a UFO was sighted and described as a bright, disc-shaped object. Pilot Thomas Mantell chased the UFO in his plane. He said it was "metallic and tremendous in size." But before he could tell any more, his plane mysteriously crashed. Searchers found Mantell dead inside the wreckage.

In 1983, a UFO was sighted over New York. According to witnesses, it had a boomerang shape, was larger than a football field, and had multicolored flashing lights. Over 5,000 people saw it, but to this day, no one knows what it was.

Are UFOS Real?

UFOS have been sighted all over the world. Some have turned out to be hoaxes. Others were meteors, aircraft, satellites, or just strange clouds. Many UFO sightings remain strange mysteries waiting to be solved.

Sometimes a strange cloud may be mistaken for a UFO.

Sometimes photos of UFOS turn out to be a hoax.

UFOs have been sighted ever since humans began recording history.

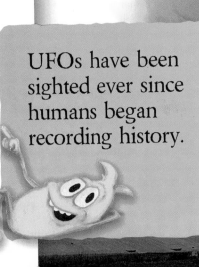

Extraterrestrials

An Extraterrestrial is something not from planet Earth. The word *extraterrestrial* is often shortened to E.T. The word *alien* is also used to describe an E.T.

Is Anyone Out There?

Many scientists believe that Earth is not the only planet with life on it. There are many millions of planets in the universe. Some of them might be just like Earth. Extraterrestrials could live on one or more of these planets.

Two Voyager spacecraft have traveled to the edge of our solar system. They carry music and greetings from Earth in case they are ever found by an extraterrestrial.

What would you say to an E.T.?

PROXIMA CENTAURI

26

Will We Ever Meet an E.T.?

Imagine meeting an E.T! It's an exciting thought, but **astronomers** don't think it's very likely. We already know there is no intelligent life in our own solar system, and the rest of the universe is much too far away to explore.

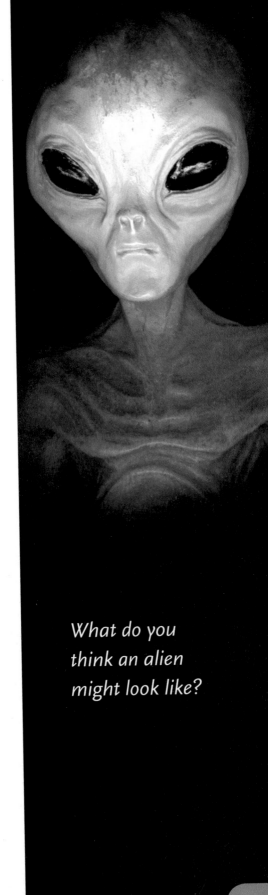

The nearest star to Earth, called *Proxima Centauri*, is 4.2 **light years** away. One light year is equal to almost 6 trillion miles (almost 9.5 trillion kilometers)! If a spaceship left Earth today, it would take 70,000 years to reach Proxima Centauri. Astronauts would not live long enough to finish the journey!

An organization called SETI (Search for Extraterrestrial Intelligence), is using powerful radio telescopes to monitor and send radio signals into outer space. Maybe one day their signals will be answered!

What do you think an alien might look like?

27

Quiz

1. The Yeti is said to live in the Himalayan Mountains.
   True/False?

2. The Loch Ness Monster is said to live in a lake in
   a) England
   b) Scotland
   c) USA
   d) Ireland

3. Atlantis is located in the Himalayas.
   True/False?

4. Stonehenge was built over
   a) 500 years ago
   b) 4,000 years ago
   c) 100 years ago
   d) 1,000 years ago

5. The Pyramids of Egypt were used as
   a) housing for the people
   b) burial places for the rulers
   c) entertainment theatres
   d) art galleries

6. A huge amount of treasure has been found on Oak Island.
   True/False?

7. What was in Beale's iron box?
   a) gold bars
   b) numbers written on paper
   c) nothing
   d) a map giving the location of the treasure

8. A UFO is an
   a) unidentified flying object
   b) undercover flight official
   c) unarmed flying object
   d) ultrasonic flying object

9. Scientists have proven that intelligent life exists in Earth's solar system.
   True/False?

10. Traveling by rocket ship, it would take _____ to reach our nearest star.
    a) 30 days
    b) six months
    c) 25 years
    d) 70,000 years

Answers

10 d)
9 False
8 a)
7 b)
6 False
5 b)
4 b)
3 False
2 b)
1 True